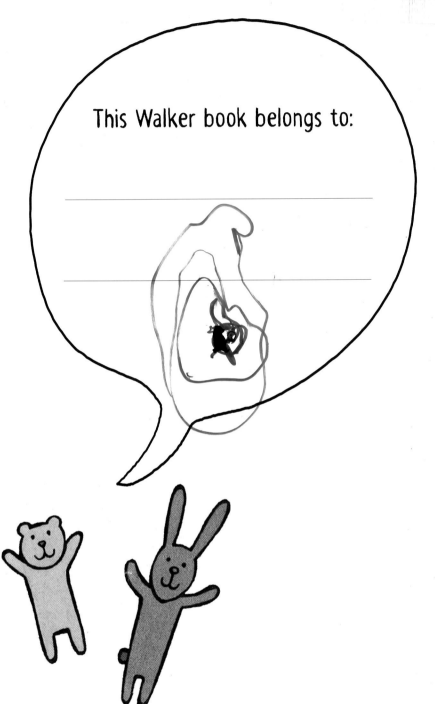

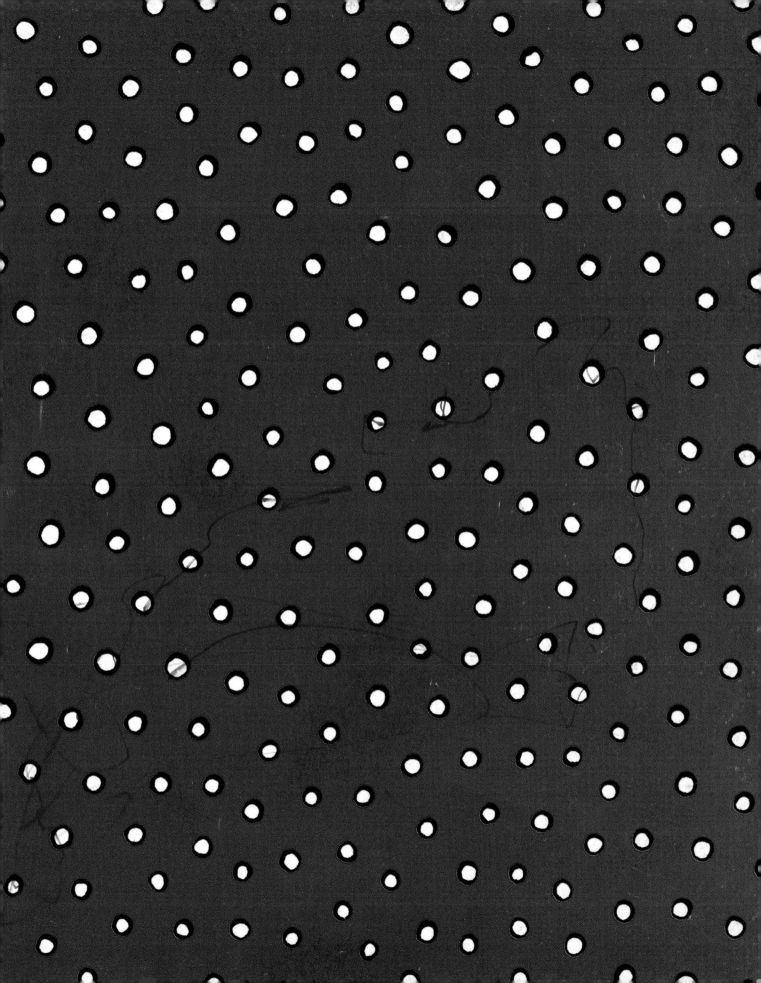

Text first published 1986
by HarperCollins Publishers Ltd
First published in 1994
by Walker Books Ltd
87 Vauxhall Walk
London SE11 5HJ

This edition first published 2008

2 4 6 8 10 9 7 5 3 1

Text © 1986 Judy Hindley
Illustrations © 1994 Nick Sharratt

The moral rights of the author
and illustrator have been asserted.

This book has been typeset in Garamond Book Educational.

Printed in China

British Library Cataloguing in Publication Data:
a catalogue record for this book is available.
from the British Library

ISBN 978-1-4063-1670-4

www.walkerbooks.co.uk

Isn't It Time?

Judy Hindley

Illustrated by

Nick Sharratt

WALKER BOOKS
AND SUBSIDIARIES

LONDON · BOSTON · SYDNEY · AUCKLAND

Tick-tock, tick-tock, tick-tock,

BLEEEP!

Wake up! Wake up!

It's seven o'clock in the morning!

Isn't it time you were up and about?

Quick, wake up!

Get up!

Get out!

Look at the sky! Look at the sun!

Look at us and Dad and Mum!

It's time to wake up at our house!

Eight o'clock, eight o'clock…

Isn't it time to go?

Around the house,

around the block,

everyone knows it's eight o'clock!

They're washing and dressing

and eating their toast,

and cleaning their shoes

and collecting their post.

It's time to be ready to go!

Nine o'clock, nine o'clock...

Isn't it time for school?

Hang up your coat!

Sit in your chair!

You know we can't start

until everyone's here,

and it's time for the buzzer to go.

BUZZ!

It's time for our school to start!

Ten o'clock, ten o'clock…

Isn't it time for milk?

Look at your hands!

Look at your face!

Wash out your brushes!

Clean up the place!

We're thirsty.

It's time for some milk!

Eleven o'clock, eleven o'clock...

Isn't it time to go out?

Isn't it time to sing and shout,

and jump and fight and rush about?

Everyone else wants to play.

Hey!

It's time to go out and play!

Twelve o'clock, twelve o'clock…

Aren't you a little bit hungry yet?

There's salad and sandwiches,

jelly and stew –

but soon there'll be nothing at all for you.

Hurry!

It's time to eat!

One o'clock, one o'clock...

Isn't it time for a rest?

Isn't it time to sit quietly down

with your feet on the floor

and your chair on the floor

and your head on your hands

on your desk?

Sshhh!

It's time for the story to start!

Two o'clock, two o'clock..

Isn't it time for a walk?

Outside in the sun,

there's a world going on,

creeping and hopping

and flying and hiding,

down in the puddles,

up in the trees,

and under the stones on the lawn.

Come on!

It's time for our nature walk!

What's the time? Look at the clock.

Three o'clock!

RUN!

Time to go home

and tidy up.

What a long day it's been!

We had to get up at seven o'clock,

and be ready to go at eight o'clock,

and start our lessons at nine o'clock,

and have our milk at ten o'clock,

and go out to play at eleven o'clock,

and eat our lunch at twelve o'clock,

and have our story at one o'clock,

and go for our walk at two o'clock,

and get very busy at three o'clock,

because … because at four o'clock –

KNOCK, KNOCK, KNOCK, KNOCK…

It's time for the party to start!

Five o'clock, five o'clock…

Isn't it time for the games to stop?

Isn't it time for the prizes now?

Isn't it time for the sweets?

Isn't it time for the birthday cake?

ISN'T IT TIME TO EAT?

Six o'clock, six o'clock…

Isn't it time for the presents?

Now!

Open them up –

What's in the box?

Tick-tock…

WOW!

So isn't it time to tell the time?

Look at it.

What does it say?

Seven o'clock, seven o'clock,

the end of a wonderful day.

Sleep well, sleep tight,

it's seven o'clock, seven o'clock,

seven o'clock

at night.

Tick-tock,

tick-tock,

tick-tick-tick-tick-tick…

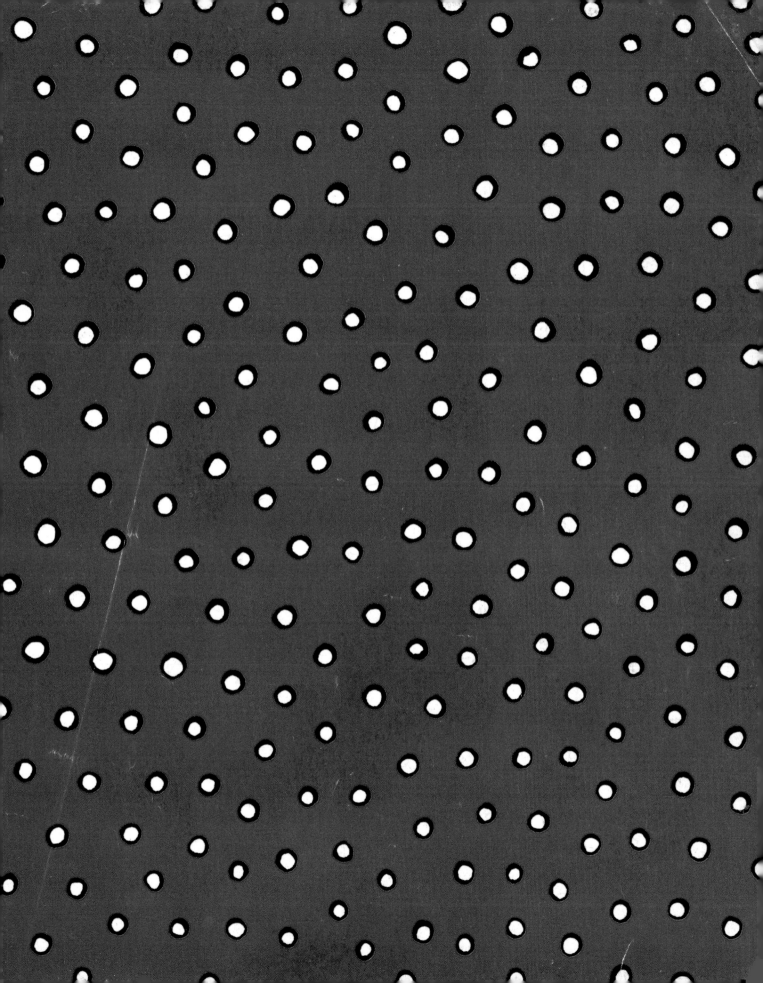

Titles in this series

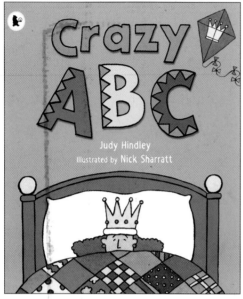

ISBN 978-1-4063-1669-8

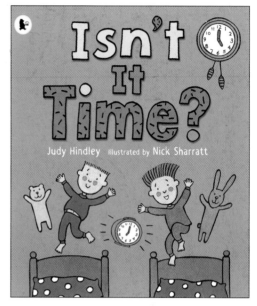

ISBN 978-1-4063-1670-4

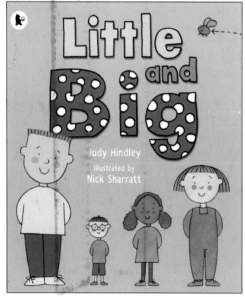

ISBN 978-1-4063-1668-1

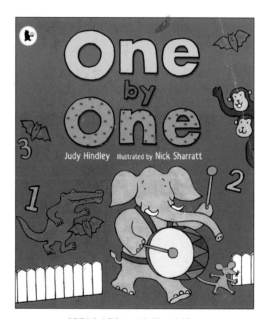

ISBN 978-1-4063-1667-4

Available from all good bookstores

www.walkerbooks.co.uk